Francesca Sinito

OPPIAN

Published by Oppian Press
Helsinki, 2020

ISBN 978-951-877-165-7

Introduction

The definition of adverb *(in Italian "avverbio")* derives from latin *"ad verbum"*, which literally means *"near the verb"*. In fact, adverbs are invariable forms that serve to modify or determine the meaning of a verb, an adjective, a clause, or another adverb, in order to give a particular meaning to the sentence. An adverb used in this way may provide information about the manner, place, time, frequency, certainty, or other circumstances of the activity. We can put adverbs at the front, in the middle or at the end of a clause, just like in English.

There are **qualifying adverbs**, that as you will see are the most numerous group, since almost all the qualifying adjectives, with the addition of **-mente**, can become adverbs of manner. In English, these adverbs usually end in **-ly** (e.g. easily, *"facilmente"*), and they act as amplifiers, which means that they make the meaning of the sentence stronger. Qualifying adverbs are usually placed at the end of the sentence, unless the adverb is the most important part of the phrase or if the object is very long.

Then, you will find **determinative adverbs**, which can be divided into 4 groups: adverbs of **time**, **place** (usually placed at the end of the sentence), **quantity** and **comparison** (usually placed after the main verb of the sentence) and they all determine a circumstance which is external to the action. Determinative adverbs are essential to give meaning to the sentence.

Furthermore, you will find **adverbs of affirmation**, used to affirm (*certamente*), **adverbs of denial**, used to deny (*nemmeno*), **adverbial adjuncts** (*anche*), used to provide additional information to a sentence and last but, by no means, least, **adverbs of doubt** (*forse*), used to express that what you're saying is uncertain.

Interrogative adverbs are also often used in Italian, and they are the "question words" used at the beginning of a question (Where are you going? *Dove vai?*) The adverbs that have been chosen are commonly used in everyday conversation and writing.

As already stated, using adverbs in a sentence is not always necessary. But when you see or hear them, not only are you getting information about the thoughts and feelings of the person who is speaking or writing, you are also learning about how strongly they feel about the topic that is being discussed.

After mastering adverbs, you will become such a great storyteller in Italian, and you'll be able to describe things more in depth. With a little practice, you'll see that adverbs are quite easy to learn and by correctly using them, your spoken and written Italian will *definitely* sound much more fluent.

Good luck!

abbastanza
enough, quite, rather, relatively, reasonably

5

Non avevamo abbastanza pane.
We didn't have enough bread.

Sono abbastanza sicuro che arriveranno presto.
I'm quite sure they will be here soon.

Il contratto è abbastanza chiaro.
The contract is rather straightforward.

Questa teoria è abbastanza semplice.
This theory is relatively easy.

Sono abbastanza soddisfatto della giornata.
I am reasonably satisfied with today.

abilmente
skilfully, cleverly, proficiently, artfully

Mio padre fronteggiò abilmente quei cani randagi.
My dad skilfully faced those stray dogs.

Il quadro fu abilmente rubato dai ladri.
The painting was cleverly stolen by the thieves.

Sa usare la sua spada giapponese abilmente.
He wields its Japanese sword proficiently.

Hanno abilmente evitato una risposta diretta.
They artfully evaded a direct answer.

Queste case sono abilmente decorate.
These houses are artfully decorated.

abitualmente
usually, typically, generally, ordinarily, frequently

I sintomi compaiono abitualmente entro 2 settimane.
Symptoms usually appear within two weeks.

La stagione estiva è abitualmente ricca di concerti.
The summer season is typically a period filled with concerts.

Le persone intelligenti sono abitualmente anche sensibili.
Smart people are generally sensitive, too.

Mio padre segue abitualmente il calcio.
My father ordinarily follows football matches.

Quest'area non è abitualmente frequentata dai cittadini.
This area is not frequently visited by the inhabitants.

addirittura
even, actually, downright, absolutely

Ti capisco addirittura, qualche volta.
I even understand you sometimes.

Vorrebbero addirittura che indossassi un'uniforme.
They even want me to wear a uniform.

Sai, potrei addirittura essermi innamorata.
You know, I think I might actually be in love.

A volte gli argomenti possono diventare addirittura cattivi.
Sometimes arguments can get downright offensive.

È una cosa addirittura senza precedenti.
This is something absolutely unheard of.

adesso
now, nowadays, presently, next, right now

Jenny, non farmi questo adesso.
Jenny, please don't do this to me now.

Una volta non si combatteva come facciamo adesso.
At one time, they didn't fight like we do nowadays.

Adesso, mi sto godendo il momento.
Presently, I'm living in the moment.

Resta la domanda su cosa faremo adesso.
The question remains as to what we do next.

Il medico lo sta controllando adesso.
The doctor is looking at him right now.

allora
then, well, therefore, so

Quest'attrice era bella già allora.
This actress was beautiful, even then.

Allora si amavano molto.
They really loved each other then.

Va bene, allora, divertiti!
All right, well, have fun!

È allora necessario capire cosa possiamo fare a riguardo.
Therefore, it is important to understand what we can do about it.

Dobbiamo allora impegnarci per sostenere l'ambiente.
We therefore have to make an effort to sustain the environment.

almeno
at least, no less than, anyway

Potrebbe almeno cercare di capire.
He could at least try to understand.

Lei almeno sa come studiare.
Well, at least she knows how to study.

Ci vorranno almeno 3 giorni per farlo.
It will take no less than 3 days to do it.

Il peggio è passato, almeno per noi.
The worst is over, for us, anyway.

Tuo fratello è intelligente almeno tanto quanto te.
Your brother is fully as smart as you are.

altrimenti
alternatively, otherwise, differently, else

Possiamo cucinare, o altrimenti ordinare del cibo d'asporto.
We can cook, or alternatively we can order take-out.

Sicuramente non sa niente, altrimenti ce lo direbbe.
He doesn't know anything, otherwise he would tell us.

Andiamo, altrimenti facciamo tardi.
Let's go, otherwise we'll be late.

Sei intelligente e non lasciare che chiunque ti dica altrimenti.
You're smart, and don't let anyone else tell you differently.

Devi rincorrerla, o altrimenti non tornerete più insieme.
You have to run after her, or else you won't get back together.

alquanto
quite, rather, pretty, fairly, extremely

La realtà può essere alquanto diversa.
Reality can be quite different.

Immagino ti sentirai alquanto confusa.
I imagine you're feeling rather confused.

Giulio sta dicendo delle cose alquanto discutibili.
Giulio is saying some pretty controversial things over there.

È una situazione alquanto particolare.
This situation is fairly particular.

Il film che guarderete è alquanto sgradevole.
The movie you're about to see is extremely unpleasant.

ancora
still, yet, again, even, more

Ti comporti ancora come un bambino.
You still act like a child.

Il rapporto non è ancora completo.
The report is not complete yet.

È un piacere rivedervi ancora.
It's a pleasure to see you again.

La prossima volta sarà ancora più divertente.
Next time will be even more fun.

Potremmo pranzare e parlare ancora.
We could have lunch and talk some more.

anche
also, even, including, likewise, too

Venne anche nominata vicepresidente.
She was also appointed as vice-president.

Sto anche incominciando a imparare il russo.
I'm even starting to learn Russian.

Siamo tutti stanchi, anche io.
We're all tired, including myself.

Potresti anche voler studiare Management.
You might likewise want to take up Management.

Sono molto contento per te, e anche per Giulia.
I'm very pleased for you, and for Giulia, too.

anzi
indeed, in fact, actually, instead, on the contrary

Questa torta non è male, anzi, è molto buona.
This cake isn't too bad, it's very good indeed.

Non l'ha perdonato, anzi l'ha quasi cacciato.
She didn't forgive him, in fact she almost kicked him out.

Non è stupido, anzi, conosce molte cose.
He's not stupid, actually, he knows a lot.

Non possiamo perdere tempo, anzi, dobbiamo fare in fretta.
We can't lose time, instead, we have to hurry.

Non me ne sono dimenticato, anzi.
I didn't forget about it, on the contrary.

anzitutto
firstly, above all, especially, mainly

Parlerò anzitutto dei lavori eseguiti.
I will firstly comment on the work carried out.

Anzitutto vorrei congratularmi con l'insegnante.
I would firstly like to congratulate the teacher.

La rivoluzione deve essere anzitutto culturale.
The revolution must be above all a cultural one.

Hai fatto importanti progressi, anzitutto nel modo di pensare.
You've made significant progress, especially in the way you think.

La catastrofe ha colpito anzitutto le classi più povere.
The disaster mainly hit the lower classes.

apertamente
openly, frankly, freely

Nessuno mi ha mai amato tanto apertamente.
I don't think I've been so openly loved by anyone before.

Devono affrontare questo fatto apertamente.
They have to face that fact openly.

Potete parlare apertamente.
You can speak frankly.

Forse non avrei dovuto renderlo parte dei miei dubbi così
apertamente.
Maybe I shouldn't have expressed my doubts so frankly to him.

Ho bisogno di parlarti apertamente.
I need to speak to you freely.

appena
just, only, barely, hardly, recently

Devo richiamarti perché Luca è appena arrivato.
I have to call you back because Luca just came in.

Sto meglio da appena due settimane.
It's only been two weeks since I'm better.

Conosco appena quest'uomo.
I barely know this man.

Ero stanchissima, riuscivo appena a parlare.
I was so tired; I could hardly speak.

Ho appena comprato una nuova macchina.
I recently bought a new car.

appunto
precisely, exactly, indeed, rightly, specifically

Tale è appunto il significato di filosofia.
This is precisely the significance of Philosophy.

Ed è appunto di quello che sto parlando.
And that's exactly what I'm saying.

Questa è appunto una caratteristica della stupidità.
This is, indeed, a peculiarity of stupidity.

Il nome scientifico scaturisce appunto da questa caratteristica.
The scientific name rightly comes from this characteristic.

Il detective è appunto incaricato di condurre le indagini.
The detective is responsible specifically to conduct investigations.

assolutamente
absolutely, totally, completely, definitely, certainly

Quello che mi chiedi è assolutamente fuori questione.
What you're asking me is absolutely out of question.

Ho lavorato tutto il giorno e sono assolutamente stremato.
I worked all day and I'm totally exhausted.

Restai assolutamente sopraffatto da questo capolavoro.
I was completely overwhelmed by this masterpiece.

Voglio assolutamente saperne di più.
I definitely want to know more about it.

Su questo hai assolutamente ragione.
You are certainly right about that.

attentamente
carefully, closely, attentively, thoroughly

Te lo spiegherò molto attentamente.
I'll explain this to you very carefully.

Dobbiamo guardare il film attentamente.
We have to watch the film closely.

Stiamo tutti ascoltando attentamente.
We are all listening attentively.

Russel dice di aver letto il foglio attentamente.
Russel says he's read the paper thoroughly.

La polizia ha perquisito la stanza attentamente.
The police searched the room very thoroughly.

avanti
forward, ahead, along

Devi guardare avanti, non indietro.
You need to look forward, not back.

Abbiamo dei progetti che stanno andando avanti.
We have a couple of projects that are moving forward.

Per favore, guarda avanti mentre guidi.
Please look ahead while you're driving.

Rinunciate al passato, e andate avanti.
Forgo the past and move along.

Vieni avanti, Giulio, e dammi un abbraccio.
Come along, Giulio, and give me a hug.

bene
well, fine, good, alright

Li conoscevo bene, molto bene.
I knew them well, very well.

Starà bene in un paio di giorni.
He'll be fine within a couple days.

È andato tutto bene e siamo arrivati a casa salvi.
Everything went well and we arrived home safe.

Ti darà l'antibiotico e controllerà che tu stia bene.
He'll give you an antibiotic and he'll see if you're alright.

Mi chiedo se stia mangiando bene.
I wonder if he's eating alright.

brevemente
briefly, shortly, concisely, succinctly

Vorrei intervenire brevemente sulla questione.
I would like to say something briefly about the matter.

Molto brevemente, osserviamo alcuni business.
Very briefly, let's look at some businesses.

Il primo capitolo descrive brevemente in cosa consiste l'azienda.
The first chapter describes shortly what the business is about.

Questo grafico riepiloga brevemente i dati raccolti.
This graphic concisely summarizes the collected data.

Fornisci brevemente tutte le informazioni richieste.
Succinctly provide all the information required.

brillantemente
brilliantly, brightly, successfully, with flying colours

26

Avevi un compito difficile e l'hai eseguito brillantemente.
You had an impossible task and you did it brilliantly.

La gara è andata brillantemente.
The race went brilliantly.

La parete è stata brillantemente colorata.
The wall was brightly coloured.

Possiamo superare brillantemente le difficoltà.
We can successfully overcome our troubles.

Sono certa che passerai l'esame brillantemente.
I'm sure you'll pass with flying colours.

certamente
certainly, surely, definitely, undoubtedly

Sa certamente badare a tuo figlio.
She can certainly look after your child.

Sembrano certamente creature da fantascienza.
These, surely, look like creatures from science-fiction.

Sa certamente come motivare le persone.
He definitely knows how to motivate people.

Lucia è certamente la miglior cantante della città.
Lucia is undoubtedly the best singer in the city.

È stato certamente il destino a farci incontrare.
It was undoubtedly fate that brought us together.

chiaramente
clearly, obviously, plainly, definitely, specifically

Insomma, è chiaramente in controllo.
I mean, he's clearly in control.

Chiaramente, non sei interessato.
Obviously, you're not interested.

Credo sia ora di parlare chiaramente.
I think it's time we speak plainly.

La risposta è no, chiaramente.
The answer is definitely no.

Per questo ho chiaramente chiesto di te.
That's why I specifically asked for you.

cioè
namely, well, that is to say

Dovremmo iniziare a utilizzare le energie sostenibili, cioè solare,
eolica, biocarburanti.
We should start using sustainable energies, namely solar power,
wind power, and biofuels.

Doveva affidarsi a chi del caso, cioè, te.
She should have left it to the professionals, namely, you.

È la mia persona preferita. Cioè, era.
He's my favourite person. Well, was.

Questo posto è… cioè, era casa mia.
This place is – well, was – my home.

Abbiamo scelto la ribellione, cioè, la vita.
We chose rebellion, that is to say, life.

ciononostante
nevertheless, however, nonetheless, notwithstanding

È scappato ma ciononostante, noi lo prenderemo.
He ran away; nevertheless, we will get him.

A sua detta la torta non le piaceva, ciononostante l'ha mangiata
tutta.
She said didn't like the cake, however, she ate all of it.

Sei un bravo ragazzo, ciononostante, ti hanno visto rubare.
You're a good boy, however, they caught you stealing.

Capisco che questo lavoro sia una punizione per lei,
ciononostante, mi aspetto una certa professionalità.
I understand this is punishment duty for you, but I expect
professional standards, nonetheless.

Ciononostante, resta ancora molto da fare per rendere questa città
sicura.
Notwithstanding, a great deal remains to be done to make this
town safe.

circa
about, approximately, roughly, nearly, almost

Ho circa un 20 giorni per prepararmi all'esame.
I have about 20 days to prepare for the exam.

Esistono circa cento miliardi di galassie nello spazio.
There are approximately a hundred billion galaxies in the
universe.

Sara ha circa 10 gatti.
Sara has roughly 10 cats.

Ho lavorato sulle navi per circa 30 anni.
I've been working on ships for nearly 30 years.

All'epoca avevo circa 10 anni.
At the time, I was almost ten years old.

come
like, how, similar, just as

Tuo figlio è come te.
Your son is like you.

Tracce storiche ci permettono di sapere come vivevano i Greci.
Historical records allow us to know how the ancient Greeks lived.

È come guidare una macchina, ma più semplice.
It's similar to driving a car, but easier.

Usare scarpe da corsa minimaliste è come correre a piedi nudi.
Using minimalist running shoes is similar to running barefoot.

Ce la faremo, come abbiamo sempre fatto.
We'll get through this, just as we always did.

completamente
completely, fully, totally, entirely, absolutely

Perderemo completamente il vantaggio della sorpresa.
We are completely losing our element of surprise.

Ho appreso completamente la lezione.
I fully understood the lesson.

Sarei completamente persa senza di te.
I'd be totally lost without you.

Non sono completamente disarmato.
I'm not entirely unarmed.

Inutile dirti che mi sembra completamente sbagliato.
I don't have to tell you how absolutely wrong that seems.

comunemente
commonly, usually, widely, popularly, ordinarily

È un cocktail comunemente chiamato Cuba Libre.
It's a cocktail commonly called Cuba Libre.

Questo gioco è comunemente conosciuto come Monopoli.
This game is usually known as Monopoli.

Questa pianta viene comunemente coltivata in Bolivia.
This plant is widely cultivated in Bolivia.

Questo punto è comunemente conosciuto come Pacifico.
This point is popularly known as "Pacific".

Questo tema è comunemente tabù.
This subject is ordinarily taboo.

comunque
nevertheless, anyway, either way, whatever, still

Si tratta comunque di cose superabili.
Nevertheless, those are thing we can deal with.

Non dovevi farlo, comunque.
You didn't have to do this, anyway.

Era comunque una scelta difficile.
It was a hard decision either way.

Comunque vada, sappi che ti voglio bene.
Whatever happens, just know that I love you.

Credo comunque che sia un imitatore.
I still think he's a copycat.

contemporaneamente
simultaneously, at once, contemporaneously, at the same time

Non mi sentivo vuoto, provavo tutto contemporaneamente.
I didn't feel empty, I felt everything simultaneously.

Stanno succedendo un po' troppe cose contemporaneamente.
We've got a couple too many things going on at once.

Sto uscendo con due ragazzi contemporaneamente.
I'm kind of dating with two guys at once.

Possiamo gestire fino a due clienti contemporaneamente.
Up to two clients can be contemporaneously managed.

Non posso capire se urlate tutti contemporaneamente.
I can't understand if you're all screaming at me at the same time.

continuamente
continuously, constantly, always, repeatedly, steadily

Gli dico di lavarsi i denti continuamente.
I continuously tell him to brush his teeth.

Sara attacca continuamente bottone con gli sconosciuti.
Sara is constantly starting conversations with strangers.

La gente mi chiede continuamente consigli.
People are always asking me for my advice.

Ho sentito questa domanda continuamente in aula.
I've heard this question repeatedly in class.

Da allora, la nostra azienda è cresciuta continuamente.
Since then, our business has grown steadily.

contrariamente
contrarily, despite, in contrast, contrary

Sappiamo, contrariamente ai decenni precedenti, che le donne
sono autosufficienti.
We know that, contrarily to past times, women are self-sufficient.

Contrariamente ai nostri auspici, non frequenta l'università.
Despite our best hopes, he didn't go to college.

Contrariamente al sistema attuale, sarebbero trasparenti.
In contrast to the current system, they would be transparent.

L'altare principale è rivolto ad ovest, contrariamente al modello
medievale.
The main altar is facing West, in contrast to the medieval model.

Contrariamente alle dicerie popolari, stettero insieme tutta la vita.
Contrary to popular rumour, they stayed together all their life.

così
therefore, thereby, thus, then, just

Hanno così deciso di sospendere le lezioni.
It was therefore decided that the lessons be suspended.

Vogliamo così lanciare un messaggio molto importante.
We want thereby to send out a very important message.

La città venne così completamente isolata.
The city was thus completely isolated.

Solo così potrai farti rispettare.
Only then will you get respect.

Non sono così magnanimo da perdonarti.
I'm just not big enough to forgive you.

davvero
really, actually, truly, seriously

Sei davvero preso da lei.
You're really into her.

Insieme potremmo davvero fare la differenza.
Together, we could actually make a difference.

Certi gesti vengono spontanei quando tieni davvero a qualcuno.
Some things come natural when you truly care about someone.

Non so davvero dove sia il parco giochi.
I truly don't know where the park is.

Ha pensato davvero che volessi fermarla.
She seriously thought I wanted to stop her.

debitamente
duly, properly, suitably, fully

Ogni cambiamento deve essere debitamente giustificato.
Every change will have to be duly motivated.

I vostri figli saranno debitamente nutriti.
Your children will be properly nourished.

L'autorità si assicurò che le azioni del criminale fossero
debitamente punite.
Authority made sure the criminal's transgressions were properly
punished.

Ora sei debitamente agghindato!
Now you're suitably dressed!

Il modulo deve essere debitamente compilato.
The form must be fully completed.

definitivamente
definitely, permanently, finally

Quella legge venne definitivamente abolita negli anni '90.
That law was definitely suppressed in the '90s.

Per i giovani è difficile legarsi definitivamente.
It's difficult for young people to commit themselves definitely.

Ci farebbe piacere se restassi definitivamente.
We would like you to stay permanently.

Tutta questa storia finirà presto, definitivamente.
All this business will be over soon, finally.

È la tua opportunità per combatterlo definitivamente.
This is your chance to finally take him down.

delicatamente
gently, delicately, carefully, softly

43

Strofina delicatamente il panno sulla vernice.
Rub the cloth gently onto the spray paint.

Riempire il foro e compattarlo delicatamente.
Fill in the soil and firm down gently.

Asciuga i piatti delicatamente.
Dry the dishes delicately.

Digli, molto delicatamente, che non c'è bisogno di essere triste.
Tell him, very carefully, there's no need to be sad.

Dovresti fare stretching delicatamente senza sentire dolore.
You should stretch softly and never feel pain.

dentro
inside, indoors, there, here

Andiamo, diamo un'occhiata lì dentro.
Come on, let's take a look inside.

Non devi tenere tutto dentro.
You mustn't hold everything inside.

Fuori fa troppo caldo, resta dentro.
It's too hot outside, stay indoors.

Abbiamo migliaia di dollari di attrezzature là dentro.
We've got thousands of dollars of equipment in there.

Dovete conoscere qualcuno che conta qua dentro.
You must know somebody who pulls the strings here.

dietro
behind, after, back, rear

45

Vediamo cosa succede dietro quelle tende.
See what's going on behind those curtains.

Indovinate cos'ho dietro la schiena.
Guess what I've got behind my back.

Diranno una bugia dietro l'altra.
They'll make up a lie after another.

Tu rimani dietro, Sara.
You'll be standing in the back, Sara.

Ora siamo dietro a tutti quanti.
We're now to the rear of everybody.

direttamente
directly, straight, right, immediately, first-hand

C'è una cosa che vorrei chiederti direttamente.
There's something I'd like to ask you directly.

Devo andare direttamente al lavoro.
I have to go straight to the office.

Portateli direttamente alla sala conferenze.
Take them right to the conference room.

Potete iscrivervi direttamente tramite il modulo d'iscrizione
online.
You can register immediately via the online registration form.

Sono lieto che tu ci abbia parlato direttamente.
I'm glad you spoke to her first-hand.

dolcemente
gently, softly, sweetly, quietly, peacefully

Lasciami riposare dolcemente sulla tua spalla.
Let me rest gently on your shoulder.

Quando asciughi la tua barba, strofinala dolcemente con un
panno.
When drying off your beard, softly rub it down with a towel.

Poche persone sanno sorridere dolcemente.
Not many people can smile sweetly.

Per favore, chiudi la porta dolcemente.
Please, close the door quietly.

Giulia vide riposare dolcemente i suoi bambini e sorrise.
Giulia saw her children sleeping peacefully and she smiled.

dopo
after, later, afterwards, thereafter

Dovresti fare la spesa dopo il lavoro.
You're supposed to go grocery shopping after work.

Potrai parlare dopo, quando si alza.
You can speak to her later, when she's up.

Questa scena è stata girata molto tempo dopo.
This scene was shot much later in the movie.

Ci vediamo dopo alla festa.
We'll meet afterwards at the party.

Poco dopo, arrivò anche mia sorella.
Shortly thereafter, my sister arrived too.

effettivamente
actually, indeed, effectively, truly, really

Non pensavo che volesse effettivamente tornare.
I never thought he would actually want to go back.

Abbiamo effettivamente ancora molta strada da fare.
Indeed, we still have much to do in this area.

Non penso che sia possibile effettivamente.
I don't think that's effectively possible.

Il Camerun è effettivamente terra di speranza per molti africani.
Camerun is truly a land of hope for many Africans.

È effettivamente necessario investire nella ricerca.
We really have to invest in research.

esageratamente
overly, exaggeratedly, excessively, wildly, ridiculously

Sara è esageratamente amichevole.
Sara is overly friendly.

La vostra cucina è esageratamente buona e abbondante.
Your cooking is exaggeratedly good and plentiful.

È un uomo esageratamente misterioso.
He's an excessively secretive man.

I numeri andavano su e giù eccessivamente.
The numbers went up and down wildly.

Questo vestito è esageratamente grande per me.
This dress is ridiculously big for me.

esattamente
exactly, precisely, right, really, specifically

Linda dice esattamente quello che pensa.
Linda say exactly what's on her mind.

Ci incontriamo tra esattamente 30 minuti.
I'll meet you in precisely 30 minutes.

Ero esattamente qui quando è arrivata.
I was right there when she arrived.

Questa casa non è esattamente elegante.
This household isn't really graceful.

Ho scritto esattamente quattro pagine.
I specifically wrote four pages.

esclusivamente
exclusively, solely, only, purely, entirely

52

Sono andato a Venezia esclusivamente per lei.
I went to Venice exclusively for her.

La squadra è formata esclusivamente da giocatori dilettanti.
The team is made up solely of amateur players.

Questa canzone è dedicata esclusivamente a voi.
This song is dedicated only to you.

È esclusivamente una questione di affari.
It's purely a business decision.

Se passerai il test o meno dipende esclusivamente da te.
Whether you'll pass the test or not is entirely on you.

estremamente
extremely, highly, exceedingly, deeply, immensely

Sei un essere umano estremamente complicato.
You're an extremely complicated human being.

È osservabile, ma estremamente imprevedibile.
It's observable, but it's highly unpredictable.

Studi come questi sono estremamente rari.
Studies like these are exceedingly rare.

Trovo il mio lavoro estremamente soddisfacente.
I find my job deeply fulfilling.

Francesco è estremamente seducente.
Francesco is immensely seductive.

eventualmente
eventually, possibly, hopefully, perhaps

Ti chiedo di avvertirmi, eventualmente tramite mail.
Please warn me, possibly by email.

Le bugie eventualmente diventano realtà.
Lies eventually become truth.

Sarebbe bello, eventualmente, iniziare a suonare.
It would be nice to, eventually, start playing.

Data l'occasione, eventualmente, possiamo aiutarvi.
Given the occasion, eventually, we can help you.

Descrivete ciò che vedete, eventualmente scattate delle foto.
Describe what you see, perhaps take some pictures.

evidentemente
evidently, obviously, clearly, apparently, plainly

La traduzione è evidentemente errata.
The translation is evidently wrong.

Non sei l'unico, evidentemente.
You're not the only one, obviously.

Sei totalmente paranoico, evidentemente.
You're totally paranoid, clearly.

Evidentemente lei non pensa la stessa cosa di me.
Apparently, she doesn't feel the same way about me.

Noi non siamo evidentemente responsabili di questo disastro.
We are plainly not responsible for this disaster.

facilmente
easily, readily, quickly, effortlessly, smoothly

Se ci coalizzassimo potremmo sopraffarli facilmente.
If we all got loose, we could overpower them easily.

I plug-in possono essere scaricati facilmente dal web.
Plug-ins are readily available for downloading from the Web.

Certe persone possono arrabbiarsi facilmente.
Some people loose their temper very quickly.

Puoi facilmente recuperare i dati persi.
You can effortlessly retrieve the lost data.

L'audio ora funziona facilmente.
The audio works smoothly now.

felicemente
happily, successfully, gladly, fortunately, joyfully

57

È bello vedere qualcuno sposato felicemente.
It's so nice to see someone happily married.

L'anno nuovo è iniziato felicemente.
The New Year began successfully.

Passerei felicemente un'eternità con te.
I would gladly spend an eternity with you.

Le realizzazioni positive felicemente non sono mancate.
Fortunately, there is no lack of positive achievements.

Si sono abbracciati e sono tornati felicemente a casa.
They embraced each other and went joyfully home.

fermamente
firmly, strongly, fully, steadily

Io tengo fermamente alle nostre tradizioni.
I hold on to our traditions firmly.

Sono fermamente convinto che dobbiamo reagire.
I firmly believe that we must take action.

Vi consiglio fermamente di iniziare a studiare.
I would strongly recommend that you start studying.

Sono fermamente intenzionato a diventare ricco.
I fully intend to become rich.

Io continuo a sostenere fermamente le mie idee.
I steadily hold on to my beliefs.

finalmente
finally, at last, eventually, now

Ho finalmente il coraggio di farlo.
I finally have the courage to do this.

Dopo 5 anni, finalmente inizio ad apprezzare il mio lavoro.
After 5 years, I am finally starting to appreciate my job.

È un vero piacere incontrarla finalmente.
It is a great pleasure to meet you at last.

Ritornò a studiare legge e finalmente diventò avvocato.
He returned to his law studies and eventually became a
magistrate.

Bene, finalmente arriviamo al punto.
Well, now we get to the point.

finora
yet, before, so far, until today

Gli animali più complessi finora apparsi sulla Terra.
The most complex animals yet to appear on Earth.

Non l'ho mai usato, finora.
I've not had the opportunity to use it before.

Non sono mai stata lontana da casa finora.
I've never been away from home before.

Sei stato fortunato finora.
You've been lucky so far.

Finora, non sapevo cosa significasse amare.
Until today, I didn't even know what it meant to love.

forse
possibly, probably, hopefully, maybe, likely

Saresti stata affascinata, forse anche commossa.
You would have been fascinated, possibly even moved.

Stasera no, Laura, ma forse domani.
Not tonight, Laura, ma probably tomorrow.

Ma insieme, forse, sarà realizzabile.
But together, hopefully, it is possible.

Forse dovresti essere più intraprendente.
Maybe you need to be more proactive.

Forse ho sbagliato a correre e mi sono fatto male.
It is likely that I run incorrectly and I hurt myself.

forte
strongly, loudly, heavily

Ho il forte sospetto che non stia dicendo la verità.
I strongly suspect that he's not telling me the truth.

Urla forte se hai bisogno di me.
Just yell loudly if you need me.

Parlavi così forte che non c'era bisogno di origliare.
You spoke so loudly, there was no need to eavesdrop.

Al primo giorno di scuola, il bambino pianse molto forte.
On his first day of school, the child cried very loudly.

Improvvisamente cominciò a piovere molto forte.
It suddenly began to rain heavily.

fortemente
strongly, highly, severely, seriously

Sospetto fortemente che ci stia mentendo.
I strongly suspect he's lying to us.

Non dovete, ma è fortemente raccomandato.
You don't have to, but it's highly recommended.

Sono fortemente allergico ai mirtilli.
I'm severely allergic to blueberries.

L'agricoltura è stata fortemente influenzata dalla siccità.
Agriculture has been seriously affected by drought.

Il responso è stato fortemente positivo.
The response has been extremely positive.

fuori
out, outside, away, outdoors

La situazione sta andando fuori controllo.
The situation is getting out of control.

Posso buttarti fuori in un secondo.
I can kick you out in a second.

Ci vediamo fuori.
We'll meet you outside.

L'ultima volta volevi tenermi fuori.
Last I heard, you wanted me to stay away.

È strano non poter mai uscire fuori.
It's weird never to be able to go outdoors.

generalmente
generally, usually, typically, normally, commonly

I bambini generalmente non ricevono tanti regali.
Boys generally don't get many presents.

Come ricercatrice, generalmente non lavoro con i pazienti.
As a researcher, I usually don't get to work with patients.

La scuola accetta generalmente bambini di 8 anni e più.
The school typically accepts students 8-years-old and more.

Generalmente non tratto così i miei studenti.
I don't normally treat my students like that.

Il pranzo rappresenta generalmente il secondo pasto della
giornata.
Lunch is commonly the second meal of the day.

gentilmente
kindly, gently, respectfully, politely

Ha gentilmente accettato di essere nostro testimone.
He's kindly agreed to be our other witness.

Vi chiederei gentilmente di non prendere quello.
Only I'd kindly ask you not to take that one.

Prendi la moneta e la inserisci gentilmente.
Take the coin and gently insert it.

Sto gentilmente chiedendo due minuti del tuo tempo.
I am respectfully asking for two minutes of your time.

Io rifiuto gentilmente l'offerta.
I politely turn down the offer.

già
already, yet, previously, enough

Se fosse per me, avrei già risolto.
If it were for me, this thing would be solved already.

Abbiamo già chiamato la polizia.
We've already called the police.

Volevamo vedere se fosse già arrivata.
We wanted to see if she'd come yet.

Ho già lavorato in un hotel.
I have previously worked in a hotel.

Mi sembrava fossi già al limite.
You looked like you had enough on your plate.

giustamente
rightly, justly, correctly, rightfully, appropriately

Sei giustamente sconvolta, ma fidati ti Riccardo.
You're upset, rightly, but have faith that Riccardo will do the right
thing.

Ti consegno il dono che hai giustamente meritato.
I give you the gift you justly deserve.

Come hai giustamente supposto, devi avere esperienza.
As you correctly have assumed, you must have experience.

Ci sono cose giustamente temo.
There are things I rightfully fear.

immediatamente
immediately, instantly, promptly, suddenly

Devo parlare con il capo immediatamente.
I need to talk to the boss immediately.

Rileveranno immediatamente ogni tentativo di mentire.
They will instantly detect any attempt to lie.

Queste iniziative devono essere attuate immediatamente.
These initiatives need to be put into place instantly.

Scusate il disturbo, ce ne andiamo immediatamente.
Sorry to bother, we will promptly leave.

Cambiò atteggiamento immediatamente.
He suddenly changed his tune.

improvvisamente
suddenly, abruptly, unexpectedly, all at once

Stavo lavorando e improvvisamente mi venne sete.
I was working and I was suddenly vey thirsty.

Siamo stati ottimi amici, ma a volte le cose finiscono
improvvisamente.
We had a great friendship, but sometimes things just end
abruptly.

Stanotte è arrivato improvvisamente un reporter.
Last night a reporter unexpectedly arrived.

Improvvisamente incominciò a piovere molto forte.
All at once it began to rain heavily.

Improvvisamente abbiamo sentito uno sparo.
All at once, we heard a shot.

incredibilmente
incredibly, unbelievably, amazingly, surprisingly

71

Questo bambino è incredibilmente bello.
This child is incredibly good-looking.

È così incredibilmente gentile con me.
She's so unbelievably nice to me.

Sarà incredibilmente difficile arrivarci a piedi.
It'll be unbelievably hard to get there by foot.

Se davvero incredibilmente bella.
You're really amazingly beautiful.

Nonostante sia avaro, può essere incredibilmente generoso.
For a cheap guy, he can be surprisingly generous.

indietro
back, behind, backwards, away, aside

Sono tornato indietro a causa della nebbia.
I came back because of the fog.

Non voltarti mai indietro.
Don't you ever look back.

Non lascio mai qualcuno indietro.
I never leave anyone behind.

È un bambino intelligente, ma è un po' indietro in scienze.
He's a brilliant child, but he's a little backward in Science.

Apri la porta, e resta indietro.
Now open the door, and stay aside.

indipendentemente
regardless of, independently, irrespective of, no matter

Andremo avanti indipendentemente dalla tua opinione.
We'll keep going regardless of your opinion.

Sara ha agito indipendentemente.
Sara took her action independently.

Raccogli più informazioni che puoi, indipendentemente dalla
qualità.
Gather whatever information you can, irrespective of quality.

Spero che riusciremo a partire, indipendentemente dalle
condizioni meteo.
I hope we'll be able to leave, irrespective of weather conditions.

Tutti, indipendentemente dallo stato sociale, devono mangiare.
Everyone, no matter their social status, has to eat.

indubbiamente
undoubtedly, certainly, definitely, indeed

74

Questa iniziativa è indubbiamente lodevole.
Undoubtedly, this initiative is praiseworthy.

Sara è indubbiamente una delle migliori studentesse della città.
Sara is undoubtedly one of the best students of the city.

Quel ragazzo è indubbiamente responsabile dell'incidente.
That guy is certainly responsible for the accident.

Hai indubbiamente più esperienza di me.
You definitely have more experience than me.

Il pianista è indubbiamente pieno di talento.
The pianist is indeed talented.

infinitamente
infinitely, endlessly, immeasurably, immensely

75

Il film sarà infinitamente più drammatico e tragico.
The movie will be infinitely more dramatic and tragic.

Doveva essere infelice, e infinitamente sola.
She must have been unhappy, and infinitely lonely.

Ci troviamo infinitamente affascinati a vicenda.
We find each other endlessly fascinating.

Il Cavaliere è infinitamente potente e immortale.
The Horseman is immeasurably powerful and immortal.

Ti sarei infinitamente grado se riordinassi la tua camera.
I'd be immensely grateful if you could tidy up your room.

inoltre
moreover, secondly, furthermore, additionally, besides

Si teme inoltre che questa cifra possa aumentare.
Moreover, it is feared that the number might increase.

Il libro afferma inoltre l'importanza del mangiare sano.
Secondly, this book underlines the importance of eating healthy.

È inoltre fondamentale rispettare i diritti umani.
Furthermore, the respect of human rights is very important.

Ha stabilito inoltre alcuni record nazionali.
Additionally, she set a number of national records.

E inoltre devo andare al lavoro.
And besides, I have to go to work.

insieme
together, jointly, altogether

Non sapevo facessimo ancora affari insieme.
I didn't know we still had business together.

Faremo insieme l'annuncio agli studenti.
We'll make the announcement to the students.

Vorrei ricordare il successo che abbiamo ottenuto insieme.
I would like to recall the success we have jointly achieved.

Dobbiamo essere responsabili della sicurezza tutti insieme.
We need to be jointly responsible for security.

Come sono contenta di vedervi qui tutti insieme.
I'm so happy to see everybody altogether.

intanto
meanwhile, meantime, however, first of all

Beh, intanto siamo ancora qui.
Well, meanwhile, we're still here.

Io andrò a fare la spesa, intanto voi potete iniziare a cucinare.
I'm going grocery shopping, meanwhile you can cook something.

Guardate pure la casa, io intanto vi aspetterò di sopra.
Take a look at the house, meantime, I'll be upstairs.

È vietato fumare in casa, intanto si può fumare sul balcone.
Smoking inside is forbidden, however, you can smoke on the
balcony.

Intanto, vorrei congratularmi per il tuo successo.
First of all, I wanted to congratulate you on your success.

invece
instead, rather, actually, meanwhile

Quest'estate verrai tu invece della mamma.
You're coming with me this summer, instead of Mother.

Preferirei avere i capelli lunghi invece dei capelli corti.
I'd rather have long hair rather than short hair.

Io, invece, sono molto contenta di averla incontrata.
Actually, I'm very pleased I have run into you.

Io invece credo che potrebbe vincere.
I actually think she could win.

Giulio si è fatto male; l'auto, invece, non aveva neanche un
graffio.
Giulio hurt himself; the car, meanwhile, was totally unmarked.

leggermente
slightly, lightly, gently, mildly, subtly

Il film è divertente e leggermente terrificante.
This movie is fun and slightly terrifying.

Montate leggermente la panna e incorporatela al resto.
Lightly whip the cream and add it to the rest.

Espirando, inarcate leggermente schiena e collo.
While exhaling, gently arch your back and neck.

Si sentiva rilassata e leggermente euforica quando recitava.
She felt relaxed and mildly euphoric when she acted.

Il motore è stato leggermente modificato.
The engine has been gently modified.

lentamente
slowly, slow, gently, quietly

81

Inspira, trattieni e lascia andare lentamente.
Breathe in, hold, and slowly let it out.

Sono una persona che impara lentamente.
I guess I'm just a slow learner.

Va bene, provo a parlare lentamente.
Alright, I will try to speak slowly.

Premi lentamente sul bottone per accenderlo.
Push the button gently to turn it on.

Intendo ripartire lentamente.
It's my intention to quietly rebuild.

magari
maybe, perhaps, probably, possibly, hopefully

Mentre sei lì, magari prendi un po' di uova.
While you're at it, maybe pick up some eggs.

Dovreste dire qualcosa sulla danza, magari.
You should say something about dance, perhaps.

Magari ha fatto un pranzo leggero.
He probably had a light lunch.

Riprenderemo il discorso, magari domani.
I'll talk to you again, possibly tomorrow.

Il pianoforte è una cosa che magari riprenderò in futuro.
I will hopefully focus on playing the piano in the future.

maggiormente
more, better, mostly, mainly, particularly

83

Vorrei poter essere maggiormente d'aiuto.
I wish I could have been more helpful.

Forse dovresti tenerlo maggiormente d'occhio.
You should think about keeping a better eye on him.

Finora ci siamo concentrati maggiormente sul design digitale.
So far, we focused mostly on digital design.

I prodotti maggiormente importati sono soia e olii.
The mainly imported products are soybeans and oils.

Quali sono i paesi che ne verranno maggiormente colpiti?
Which countries which will be particularly affected?

mai
possibly, never, anything, ever

Non potrei mai rinunciare al cioccolato.
I couldn't possibly give up chocolate.

Ezio non sgrida mai i suoi bambini.
Ezio never scolds his children.

Non mi sono mai innamorato.
I never fell in love.

Non gli farei mai del male.
I wouldn't do anything to hurt him.

Non guardatevi mai indietro.
Don't you ever look back.

male
wrongly, badly, amiss, unkindly

Lei è stato informato male.
You've been wrongly informed.

Il cervello funziona male senza riposo.
The brain slips badly with no rest.

Un po' di fiducia non farebbe male.
A little faith wouldn't go amiss.

Ci sono rimasto molto male.
I took it very much amiss.

Non l'ho mai sentita parlare male di qualcuno.
I never heard her speak unkindly about anyone.

meglio
better, best, well

Sara voleva capire meglio le lingue morte.
Sara wanted a better understanding of dead languages.

Mi piacerebbe conoscerti meglio.
I would very much like to know you better.

Lascia stare, sarà meglio per tutti.
Just leave it, it will be the best for everyone.

Credo sia meglio chiudere la porta.
I think it's best if we close the door.

Pensavo fossi qui per stare meglio.
I thought you were here to get well.

minimamente
minimally, remotely, whatsoever, at all

87

Ha rifiutato di provare una tecnica minimamente invasiva.
He refused to try a minimally invasive technique.

Non sono minimamente qualificato per stare qui.
I'm not remotely qualified to be here.

Questo libro non dice niente di minimamente profondo.
This book doesn't say anything remotely profound.

Giulia non si ricordava minimamente di questa storia.
Giulia had no recollection of the story whatsoever.

La cosa non mi muove minimamente.
It doesn't bother me at all.

molto
very, much, really, pretty

Giulia rende molto difficile concentrarsi sul lavoro.
Giulia is making it very hard to concentrate on my work.

È molto importante essere organizzati.
It's very important to be organized.

Chi perdona molto, ama molto.
Who forgives much, loves much.

Luca è molto simpatico.
Luca is really funny.

Sei una ragazza molto comprensiva.
You're a pretty understanding sort of girl.

naturalmente
naturally, obviously, certainly

È meglio aspettare che le cose accadano naturalmente.
It's much better to wait until things happen naturally.

Non guardanti indietro, cammina naturalmente.
Don't walk back, just walk out naturally.

Naturalmente questo non è sufficiente.
Obviously, that is not enough.

A volte dobbiamo fare delle scelte, naturalmente.
Sometimes we have to make choices, certainly.

Ho naturalmente apprezzato il suo contributo ponderato.
I certainly appreciated his considered contribution.

nemmeno
barely, hardly, either, nowhere, never

Non ci si può nemmeno muovere qui.
You can barely move here.

Non mi ero nemmeno accorta che fosse sparito.
I hardly noticed he was missing.

Non ti serve nemmeno una penna.
You don't need a pen, either.

Non siamo nemmeno vicini al mare.
We're nowhere near the ocean.

Farò qualcosa che non puoi nemmeno credere possibili.
I'll do some things you could never imagine possible.

normalmente
normally, usually, typically, generally

Abbiamo richiuso la ferita e dovrebbe guarire normalmente.
We closed the would and it should heal normally.

Non è qualcosa che faresti, normalmente.
It's not something you would normally do.

La camicia che indosso normalmente è sparita.
The blouse I usually wear has disappeared.

Il corpo normalmente si abitua in una settimana.
The body typically adapts in one week.

La consegna avviene normalmente in 2-5 giorni.
Delivery generally takes 2-5 days.

nuovamente
again, back, newly, afresh, anew

92

Non gli permetterò di farlo nuovamente.
I won't let him do that again.

Siamo diretti nuovamente a Londra.
We are headed back to London.

La villa fu decorata nuovamente nel 1.800.
The villa was decorated newly in the 1,800.

Voglio iniziare nuovamente con te.
I want to start afresh with you.

Sono guarita e sono pronta a ricominciare nuovamente.
I am healed, ready to begin anew.

ogni tanto
sometimes, occasionally, every now and then

93

Sei davvero intelligente, ogni tanto.
You're very smart, sometimes.

Per favore, mettiti al primo posto ogni tanto.
Just please put yourself first, sometimes.

Mi piacerebbe andare in palestra ogni tanto.
I'd like to go to the gym occasionally.

Ogni tanto siamo fortunati!
I guess every now and then we get lucky!

Ogni tanto ritorno al mio paese.
Every now and then I return to my country.

oltre
over, besides, in addition, further

Siamo intrappolati qui da oltre otto ore.
We've been trapped in here for over eight hours.

Qualsiasi cosa sia successa, puoi andare oltre.
Whatever happened, you can get over it.

Ci sono altre carriere oltre alla danza.
There are other careers besides dancing.

Oltre a pattinare sul ghiaccio, mi piace fare arrampicata.
In addition to ice-skating, I like rock-climbing.

Non dobbiamo parlarne oltre, Mario.
No need to discuss it further, Mario.

ormai
now, already, anymore, nowadays

Avrà circa novant'anni, ormai.
He'll be in his early nineties now.

Siamo qui da 8 settimane ormai.
We've been here for 8 weeks already.

In realtà ormai divento ansioso raramente.
In fact, I rarely get anxious anymore.

Poche persone vengono qui, ormai.
Not a lot of people come here anymore.

Ci sono così tanti incidenti ormai.
There are so many accidents nowadays.

ovviamente
obviously, naturally, clearly, certainly, evidently

È ovviamente ancora innamorato di Paola.
He's obviously still in love with Paola.

Tu andrai con lui al concerto, ovviamente.
You'll go to the concert with him, naturally.

Tutti voi avete ovviamente lavorato sodo.
You all have clearly put in a lot of work.

Questi problemi possono ovviamente essere risolti.
These problems can certainly be solved.

Chiunque l'abbia votato ovviamente era d'accordo con te.
Whoever voted him evidently agreed with you.

ora
today, nowadays, currently

Stiamo per concludere quando cominciato oggi.
We are close to finishing what we started today.

Oggi sono quasi caduto.
And today I almost keeled over.

È difficile educare i figli oggi.
It's so hard to raise children nowadays.

Non vengono scritti molti romanzi oggi.
Not many people write novels nowadays.

La regione è oggi abitata da giovani imprenditori.
The region is currently inhabited by young entrepreneurs.

ordinariamente
ordinarily, routinely, usually

Trascorro il mio tempo ordinariamente, come tutti.
I spend my time ordinarily, like anyone else.

Questo vaccino è usato ordinariamente per il morbillo.
This vaccine is routinely used for measles.

Il microscopio è ordinariamente costituito da più parti funzionali.
A microscope is usually composed of more functional parts.

Ordinariamente esco subito dopo pranzo.
I usually go outside after lunch.

I travestimenti ordinariamente richiedono parrucche e trucco.
Costumes ordinarily require wigs and make up as part of the
outfit.

parecchio
pretty, really, quite, rather

Oggi mi sento parecchio triste.
Today I feel pretty sad.

Sono parecchio arrabbiata e devi andartene.
I'm really angry and you need to go.

Luca dice cose parecchio strane a volte.
Luca says really weird stuff sometimes.

Sono parecchio curioso di vedere cosa porterà la serata.
I'm quite curious as to what the evening will bring.

Giulia ha lasciato l'aeroporto parecchio velocemente.
Giulia left the airport rather quickly.

parimenti
equally, likewise, similarly

È parimenti importante garantire che queste risorse siano usate correttamente.
It is equally important to ensure that these financial resources are being correctly deployed.

Sono due aspetti essenziali, diversi ma parimenti importanti.
These are two fundamental aspects, they're different but equally important.

Le sue risposte agli insegnanti sono state parimenti pertinenti.
Your answers to the teachers were likewise pertinent.

È parimenti evidente la necessità di rispettare i diritti umani.
Similarly, it is self-evident that we should respect human rights.

Paesi come Russia e Cina hanno luoghi parimenti stupendi.
Countries such as Russia and China have similarly beautiful places.

particolarmente
particularly, especially, highly, extremely, unusually

So di non essere particolarmente apprezzato.
I'm aware I'm not particularly well liked.

Mi sono particolarmente affezionata a voi.
I've become especially fond of you.

È un tour che raccomandiamo particolarmente.
This is a highly recommended tour.

Per lui dev'essere un momento particolarmente complicato.
This must be an extremely difficult moment for him.

Sembri particolarmente sconvolto da questa conversazione.
You seem unusually upset by this discussion.

perfettamente
perfectly, fully, completely, absolutely, beautifully

Posso assicurarle che è tutto legale, signora Joys.
It's all perfectly legal, I can assure you, Mrs Joys.

Capisco perfettamente la gravità della mia situazione.
I fully appreciate the seriousness of my situation.

Capisco perfettamente e mi dispiace davvero.
I completely understand and I'm very sorry.

Capisco perfettamente la tua posizione.
I absolutely understand where you're coming from.

Queste scarpe si sposano perfettamente con il mio blazer.
These shoes would go beautifully with my blazer.

perlopiù
mostly, mainly, primarily, largely, predominantly

Sono perlopiù dicerie, Giulia.
These are mostly rumours, Giulia.

Si dedicò perlopiù alla filosofia.
He mostly devoted himself to Philosophy.

I vini provengono perlopiù da vitigni italiani.
The wines come primarily from Italian grapes.

La nostra è una conoscenza perlopiù superficiale.
Ours is a largely superficial knowledge.

Tutte le prove vengono effettuate sugli animali, perlopiù conigli.
All such testing is currently carried out on animals,
predominantly rabbits.

però
nevertheless, nonetheless, well

Si deve però guardare al futuro.
Nevertheless, we need to look to the future.

È vero però che la situazione sembra preoccupante.
It is true, nevertheless, that the situation is worry.

La relazione solleva però alcune questioni fondamentali.
Nonetheless, the report raises fundamental issues.

È però essenziale essere sinceri.
It is nonetheless important to be honest.

In questo però non posso aiutarla.
Well, I can't provide you with any help.

personalmente
personally, firsthand, privately

Voglio parlarle personalmente di suo figlio.
I want to speak to you personally about your son.

Mi occuperò di questo io personalmente.
I'm going to take care of this personally.

Avete visto personalmente come risolvere il problema.
You saw first-hand how to solve the problem.

Voglio incontrarla personalmente.
I want to meet you privately.

Avrai il privilegio di sperimentare il tuo lavoro personalmente.
You'll have the privilege of experiencing the work firsthand.

pienamente
fully, completely, entirely, totally, wholly

Sono pienamente soddisfatto del mio lavoro.
I'm fully satisfied with my job.

Comprendo pienamente il tuo punto di vista.
I completely see eye to eye with you.

Non è pienamente corretto, così.
That is not entirely correct, like that.

Sarai pienamente soddisfatto, te lo garantisco.
You'll be totally satisfied, I guarantee it.

Sono pienamente consapevole delle mie abilità.
I am wholly aware of my capabilities.

piuttosto
rather, pretty, quite, instead, fairly

Sono piuttosto fiero del mio lavoro.
I'm rather proud of my job.

Devo ammettere che è piuttosto sorprendente.
I've got to admit, it's pretty amazing.

Alla fine, i calcoli furono piuttosto semplici.
In the end, the calculation was quite simple.

Ma parliamo di voi, piuttosto.
But let's talk about you, instead.

Mi sembra una domanda piuttosto diretta.
I think it's a fairly straightforward question.

poco
just, soon, poorly, slightly, hardly

Il viaggio è durato poco più di quattro ore.
The journey took just over four hours.

Il manager sarà qui tra poco.
The manager will be here soon.

Ci sono tante strade deserte e poco illuminate.
There are so many deserted streets, and poorly lit.

Il lavoro richiederà mezza giornata, o poco meno.
The work will require half a day, or slightly less.

Lo vedo poco al di fuori della scuola.
I hardly see him outside of school.

poi
eventually, then, next, finally

Però poi ho dovuto fare delle audizioni.
But eventually I had to hold auditions.

Tutte le mail vennero poi inoltrate al direttore.
All of the emails were eventually forwarded to the manager.

Finisci la merendina, poi parliamo.
Finish your snack, then we'll talk.

Cosa accadde poi rimane un mistero.
What happened next remains a mystery.

Non è, poi, da dimenticare il grande tema della malattia.
Finally, the great theme of disease cannot be ignored.

praticamente
virtually, basically, nearly, barely

La tecnologia sta praticamente rivoluzionando ogni settore.
Technology is bringing disruption to virtually every industry.

L'hanno praticamente minacciata.
She was basically threatened.

Mi hai praticamente detto di aspettarti.
You basically told me to wait for you.

La mia macchina è potente praticamente quanto la tua.
My car is nearly as powerful as yours.

Senza cravatta, Giulio è praticamente irriconoscibile.
Without tie, Giulio is barely recognizable.

precedentemente
previously, formerly, earlier, before, already

Vorrei ritirare la dichiarazione precedentemente fatta.
I wish to retract the statement I had previously made.

Il vulcano era precedentemente considerato estinto.
The volcano was formerly considered to be extinct.

Consulterò gli appunti che ho scritto precedentemente.
I will look at the notes which I made earlier.

L'avevo vista con lui precedentemente.
I've seen her with him before.

È scritto nella lista che vi ho precedentemente dato.
It's written in the list I've already given you.

presto
soon, early, quickly, shortly

So che troveremo presto una casa.
I know we'll find a house soon.

Il capo tornerà presto, siediti.
The boss will be back soon, sit down.

Alcuni di noi devono essere al lavoro presto.
Some of us have to be at work early.

Tu preoccupati di guarire e tornare presto.
You worry about getting better and come back quickly.

Siamo fiduciosi che lo sostituiremo presto.
We're confident we'll replace him shortly.

prima
early, before, prior, earlier, previously

Sono tornata prima per riposare un po'.
I came back early to have a bit of rest.

Facemmo un patto prima della partenza.
We made a deal before leaving.

Devi bere un frullato prima del work-out.
You need to drink a smoothie prior to working out.

Non siamo riusciti a rintracciarla prima.
We couldn't inform her earlier.

È una donna che non ho mai visto prima.
It's a woman with whom I haven't previously been acquainted.

probabilmente
probably, likely, possibly, arguably, supposedly

Tenere il gatto con noi è probabilmente una pessima idea.
Keeping the cat with us is probably a bad idea.

Se non collabora, probabilmente l'accuseranno di reticenza.
If he doesn't cooperate, they're likely to indict him on obstruction.

Sono concentrato su grandi obiettivi, probabilmente
irraggiungibili.
I'm focused on large, possibly unattainable goals.

Questo fu probabilmente il loro miglior film.
This was arguably their best film together.

Questo romanzo probabilmente è basato su una storia vera.
The novel is supposedly based on a true story.

prontamente
promptly, quickly, immediately, swiftly

Compila il foglio e sarai contattato prontamente.
Fill out the form and we will contact you promptly.

Sapevamo di dover reagire prontamente.
We knew we had to react quickly.

La mia richiesta fu prontamente accolta.
My request was quickly granted.

In caso di mancata disponibilità, il cliente sarà prontamente
informato.
In case a product is not available, the customer will be informed
immediately.

Dovremmo agire prontamente.
We should act swiftly.

proprio
really, precisely, exactly, actually

Molti dei corsi sono proprio difficili.
A lot of the courses are really tough.

È proprio quello che vogliamo scoprire.
That is precisely what we want to find out.

Mi piaci proprio per questo, Nicole.
This is exactly why I love you, Nicole.

Me l'ha confermato proprio stamattina.
She confirmed it to me exactly this morning.

Non credo sia proprio così.
I don't think that's actually right.

psicologicamente
psychologically, mentally, emotionally

A volte divento psicologicamente pigro.
Sometimes I become psychologically idle.

È una domanda psicologicamente valida.
This is a psychologically valid question.

È meglio che ti prepari psicologicamente.
You must be mentally prepared.

È psicologicamente diverso dai ragazzi della sua età.
He's emotionally unusual for a boy his age.

Credi che lo segnerà psicologicamente?
Do you think he'll be scarred emotionally?

pure
also, likewise, too, along, though

Scoprite pure cos'altro ci nasconde.
Also, find out what else he's hiding from us.

Egli mi procurò pure una guida.
He likewise procured me a guide.

Ha pure cambiato i nomi ai personaggi.
He had likewise changed the names of the characters.

Scusami, dobbiamo dire pure questo.
Sorry, we have to say that, too.

Venga pure, sig. Lucio.
Come along, Mr. Lucio.

purtroppo
unfortunately, sadly, regrettably, unhappily

Lara è intelligente, ma purtroppo sa essere molto infantile.
Lara is smart, but unfortunately, she can also be quite a child.

Ci sono cattive notizie, purtroppo.
We received bad news, unfortunately.

Purtroppo, dobbiamo restare qui.
Sadly, we have got to stay here.

Aveva altre questioni urgenti, purtroppo.
He had other obligations, regretfully.

Molti matrimoni purtroppo finiscono male.
Many marriages, unhappily, end badly.

quasi
almost, nearly, about, hardly, virtually

Non sappiamo quasi niente di queste creature.
We know almost nothing about these creatures.

È stata quasi sbattuta fuori dal programma.
She was nearly kicked out of the program.

Sono quasi in tribunale.
I'm about to head to court.

Non vedo quasi mai i miei nonni.
I hardly ever see my grandparents.

Le provviste sono quasi finite, dobbiamo fare spesa.
The food is virtually gone, we have to go grocery shopping.

rapidamente
quickly, rapidly, fast, swiftly, briefly

Dobbiamo identificare rapidamente queste persone.
We need to identify these people quickly.

Purtroppo, il denaro sta finendo rapidamente.
Unfortunately, the money is rapidly running out.

Sei giovane e cresci molto rapidamente.
You're young and you're growing really fast.

Dobbiamo procedere rapidamente, senza parlare.
We need to proceed swiftly, without talking.

Mi richiamo rapidamente a cinque punti.
I would like to briefly refer to five points.

raramente
rarely, infrequently, occasionally, scarcely, uncommonly

Mi parlava raramente dei suoi casi.
He rarely talked to me about any of his cases.

Il freddo intenso si presenta raramente nella valle.
Frost occurs infrequently in the valley.

Alcuni intervengono raramente, altri di continuo.
Some people talk occasionally, some continuously.

Queste persone raramente condividono informazioni.
These people share information scarcely.

Questa malattia può raramente essere grave.
This condition can rarely be severe.

realmente
really, actually, truly, genuinely, factually

Non sapevo come fossi realmente.
I didn't know what you were really like.

Non sappiamo se sia realmente migliore.
We don't know if he's actually better.

Giovanni è l'unico che potrebbe realmente sfidarmi.
Giovanni is the only one who could truly challenge me.

Sembrava realmente offeso dalle tue parole.
He seemed genuinely upset by your words.

In questo momento le nostre frontiere sono realmente aperte.
We factually have open borders right now.

recentemente
recently, newly, lately

Ho avuto la fortuna di incontrare Sara recentemente.
I was most fortunate to make her acquaintance recently.

Ho preso un po' di peso recentemente.
I recently gained a bit of weight.

L'appartamento è stato costruito recentemente.
The apartment is newly built.

Abbiamo dovuto affrontare parecchi cambiamenti, recentemente.
We've been dealing with a lot of changes, lately.

Sono finito in un sacco di guai recentemente.
I've been getting into a lot of trouble recently.

regolarmente
regularly, routinely, consistently, properly

Mia nonna deve prendere delle pastiglie regolarmente.
My grandma has to take tablets regularly.

Riceviamo regolarmente diverse comunicazioni.
We routinely receive various communications.

Questi esami devono essere eseguiti regolarmente.
These exams must be done routinely.

Dovrebbe lavorare regolarmente.
He should work consistently.

Se mangia regolarmente e riposa, si rimetterà.
If he eats properly and rests, he'll be fine.

relativamente
relatively, comparatively, regarding, fairly, reasonably

Credo sia relativamente semplice fare una buona canzone.
I think that it's relatively easy to create a good song.

Si tratta di una procedura relativamente nuova.
This is a comparatively new procedure.

Maggiori dettagli relativamente alle prenotazioni saranno
disponibili a breve.
More details regarding booking will soon be available.

Tuttavia, il rischio sembra essere relativamente basso.
However, the risk seems to be fairly low.

Possiamo essere relativamente soddisfatti.
We can be reasonably satisfied.

semplicemente
simply, merely, easily, purely

Sono semplicemente un musicista, niente di più.
I'm simply a musician, nothing more.

Avrebbe potuto trattarti semplicemente di un parente.
It is possible that he was merely a relative.

Il suo appetito potrebbe semplicemente trattarsi di una carenza
nutrizionale.
Her unusual appetite may merely indicate a nutrient deficiency.

Questa situazione può essere rivolta molto semplicemente.
This situation can be sorted out really easily.

È stata semplicemente legittima difesa, te lo assicuro.
It was purely self-defense, I assure you.

sempre
always, ever, constantly, still

Hai sempre nascosto la tua vera identità.
You've always hidden your true identity.

Ti trovo bellissima, come sempre.
You look just as beautiful as ever.

Vengo sempre umiliato perché non ho soldi.
I'm constantly humiliated because I don't have any money.

Ho sempre bisogno di fare qualcosa.
I have to be doing something, constantly.

Sei sempre molto bravo ai ricevimenti.
You're still very good at cocktail parties.

sicuramente
definitely, certainly, surely, undoubtedly, probably

È un libro che leggerei sicuramente.
It's a book I would definitely read.

Avrebbe potuto sicuramente ferirmi.
He certainly could have hurt me.

Ci sarà sicuramente qualcosa che desidera.
There must be something she surely desires.

Mi sembra sicuramente un obiettivo molto importante.
In my view this is undoubtedly a very important objective.

Starà sicuramente andando a scuola.
She's probably headed to school.

silenziosamente
silently, quietly, softly, soundlessly

I serpenti si muovono silenziosamente.
Snakes move silently.

Provò a baciare Lucia, ma lei lo respinse silenziosamente.
He tried to kiss Lucia, but she silently rejected him.

Entra silenziosamente e siediti alla mia scrivania.
Enter quietly and sit down at my desk.

Penso a lui e piango silenziosamente nell'angolo.
I reminisce about him and cry softly in the corner.

Le sue labbra si muovono silenziosamente in preghiera.
His lips move soundlessly in prayer.

sinceramente
honestly, sincerely, frankly, truly, genuinely

Ti sto parlando sinceramente.
I'm trying to speak to you honestly.

Mi scuso sinceramente per averle causato imbarazzo.
I sincerely apologize for embarrassing you in any way.

Sinceramente, non so cosa dire.
Frankly, I don't know what to say.

Ti amerò sempre, sinceramente e profondamente.
I will love you always, truly and deeply.

Sono sinceramente preoccupato per lei.
I'm genuinely worried about her.

solamente
only, merely, solely, simply, purely

Useremo solamente i migliori ingredienti.
We will only use the finest ingredients.

L'ho solamente ammirata da lontano.
I have merely admired her from a distance.

Si focalizzarono solamente sui dipinti.
They focused solely on the paintings.

Desidero solamente mangiare.
I simply wish to eat.

La nostra presenza qui è solamente temporanea.
Our presence here is purely temporary.

solitamente
generally, usually, typically, normally, commonly

Le persone che vengono tradite solitamente non perdonano.
People who get cheated on don't generally forgive.

Solitamente facciamo un incontro con i genitori.
We usually have a meeting with the parents.

Solitamente, in caso di allergia, ci sono vari modi di risolvere il
problema.
Usually, in case of allergy, there are two ways of solving the
problem.

Le sessioni pomeridiane sono solitamente riservate ai membri del
club.
Afternoon sessions are normally reserved for our club members.

Le costruzioni egizie sono solitamente conosciute come piramidi.
Egyptian constructions are commonly known as Pyramids.

solo
just, merely, simply, solely

Cercavo solo di dire le cose come stavano.
I was just trying to keep the facts straight.

Le giuro che stavamo solo parlando.
We were merely talking, I swear.

Stavo solo avanzando una critica costruttiva.
I was simply offering some constructive criticism.

Sto solo cercando di raggiungere questo obiettivo.
I'm simply trying to reach that goal.

Preferirei ricevere direttive solo da te.
I'd prefer to receive directions solely from you.

soltanto
only, simply, exclusively, purely

Posso consegnare questa lettera soltanto alla Sig.ra Rosa.
I can only deliver this letter to Mrs. Rosa.

Un ritratto costa soltanto 5 euro.
I only charge 5 euros for a portrait.

Ci tenevo soltanto a informare i miei colleghi.
I simply wished to inform my fellow colleagues.

Non farei nulla soltanto per denaro.
I would do nothing purely for money.

Le armi sono soltanto per sicurezza.
The weapons are purely for security.

soprattutto
especially, particularly, mainly, mostly

Questo posto è bellissimo, soprattutto al tramonto.
This place is beautiful, especially at sunset.

Non voglio ascoltare niente, soprattutto musica rock.
I don't want to listen to anything, especially rock music.

Era abile soprattutto con le lingue straniere.
He was particularly good at foreign languages.

Dal 2002 lavora soprattutto come traduttrice.
Since 2002 she mainly works as a translator.

Ero arrabbiata, ma soprattutto preoccupata.
I was angry, but mostly worried.

specialmente
especially, particularly, notably, mostly, specifically

Perderai tutti i tuoi amici, specialmente Daniel.
You will lose all your friends, especially Daniel.

Esprimo questo auspicio specialmente pensando ai giovani.
I express this hope particularly with the young in mind.

Alcune lingue, specialmente il russo, sono considerate difficili.
Some foreign languages, notably Russian, are considered hard.

Questi animali vivono specialmente nella regione artica.
These animals mostly live in the arctic.

Alcuni materiali, specialmente ceramiche, si rompono facilmente.
Some materials, specifically ceramics, can easily break.

spesso
often, frequently, usually, commonly, regularly

Vai a trovare tua nonna molto spesso.
You visit your grandmother very often.

Mia mamma suonava spesso la chitarra.
My mom frequently played the guitar.

Non capita spesso di vedere daini da queste parti.
We don't usually see deer down here.

I bambini più timidi vengono spesso esclusi.
Shy children are very commonly left out.

Laura va spesso al cinema.
Laura goes to the cinema regularly.

subito
immediately, quickly, right now, soon

Con la vostra autorizzazione, possiamo iniziare subito.
If you give your permission, we could begin immediately.

Contatterò subito Darius.
I'll contact Darius immediately.

Sono tornata subito perché continuavi a chiamarmi.
I came back quickly because you were driving me crazy with your
calls.

Andrew, dimentica tutto, subito.
Andrew, forget everything, right now.

Dobbiamo andarcene via subito.
We should be getting out of here soon.

successivamente
later, subsequently, afterwards, thereafter

Giulio successivamente divenne avvocato.
Giulio later became a magistrate.

La città acquisì successivamente importante per il turismo.
The city gained subsequently significance thanks to tourism.

Questi prodotti vengono testati successivamente in laboratorio.
Afterwards, these products are tested in the laboratory.

I miei nonni si sposarono e successivamente vissero a Verona.
My grandparents married and lived thereafter in Verona.

La nave fu successivamente demolita.
The ship was eventually broken up.

sufficientemente
sufficiently, enough, fairly, reasonably

È preoccupato che non siamo sufficientemente preparati.
He's concerned we're not sufficiently prepared.

La questione demografica non è sufficientemente trattata.
The issue of overpopulation is not sufficiently dealt with.

Dovrai essere sufficientemente convincente.
You'll have to be convincing enough.

Il prodotto è sufficientemente resistente.
This is a fairly hardy product.

Il tuo discorso è sufficientemente incoraggiante.
Your speech is reasonably encouraging.

talvolta
sometimes, occasionally, at times, often

Talvolta puoi essere incredibilmente cinica.
Sometimes you can be curiously unfeeling.

Comprendo che talvolta sia difficile ricordarselo.
I realize sometimes it's hard to remember.

Talvolta pensa anche a studiare.
He occasionally thinks about studying.

Silvio era talvolta rattristato, ma mai scoraggiato.
Silvio was at times saddened, but never discouraged.

Una volta, la tubercolosi era talvolta associata al vampirismo.
At one time, tuberculosis was often associated with vampires.

tranquillamente
quietly, safely, easily, calmly, peacefully

I miei nonni vissero tranquillamente su una collina.
My grandparents lived quietly on a hill.

Possiamo tranquillamente dire che non ha funzionato.
We can safely say that it didn't work.

È una cosa che puoi tranquillamente fare su internet.
It's something you can easily do on the internet.

Sono convinta che accetterà la cosa tranquillamente.
I'm convinced she'll accept the news calmly.

Sta dormendo così tranquillamente!
He's sleeping so peacefully!

troppo
excessively, overly, little, awfully

Sei un musicista troppo esperto.
You're an excessively skilled musician.

Forse sono un po' troppo ambizioso.
Maybe I'm a little overly ambitious.

Penso tu sia troppo critico.
I think you're being overly critical.

Sei stato troppo tranquillo finora.
You're being awfully quiet right now.

Lei è troppo gentile, signore.
This is awfully kind of you, Sir.

tuttavia
however, nevertheless, nonetheless, although

È tuttavia necessario svolgere ulteriori indagini.
It is however necessary that further surveys be carried out.

Sembra tutta via necessaria una precisazione.
Nevertheless, there seems to be a need for clarification.

L'economia, tuttavia, deve ancora stabilizzarsi.
The economy, nonetheless, still needs to be stabilized.

Vorrei tuttavia soffermarmi su una questione più urgente.
Nonetheless, I wish to come back to a more urgent issue.

Ho portato dei dolci semplici, tuttavia gustosi.
I brought some simple cakes, although tasty.

tuttora
still, today, now, currently

Rifiutano tuttora di comunicare.
They still refuse to communicate.

Sono tuttora sconcertata dal suo comportamento.
I'm still baffled by his behaviour.

È una battaglia che combattiamo tuttora.
It's a battle we're fighting today.

Ha costruito la casa nella quale tuttora viviamo.
He built the house that we now live in.

Il torneo è tuttora sponsorizzato da quell'azienda.
The tournament is currently sponsored by that entreprise.

ugualmente
equally, likewise, anyway, similarly

È importante trattare le persone ugualmente.
It's imperative to treat people equally.

Il sole stesso può ugualmente uccidere.
The sun itself can likewise kill.

Sappiamo ogni cosa l'uno dell'altro e ci amiamo ugualmente.
We know everything about each other and we love each other
anyway.

Sara non vuole venire, ma la convincerò ugualmente.
Sara doesn't want to come, but I'll convince her anyway.

Non ha molte speranze, ma vuole tentare ugualmente.
He doesn't have many hopes, but he wants to try similarly.

ulteriormente
further, additionally, ulteriorly, any longer.

Non vorremmo rischiare di traumatizzarlo ulteriormente.
We wouldn't want to risk getting him further traumatized.

Questo rafforza ulteriormente la mia ipotesi.
This further strengthens my hypothesis.

Acquistare all'ingrosso riduce ulteriormente la spesa complessiva.
You can buy in bulk, which additionally reduces the total expense.

Questo oggetto merita di essere studiato ulteriormente.
This object has to be studied ulteriorly.

Signore, non possiamo ritardare ulteriormente.
Sir, we cannot delay any longer.

ultimamente
lately, recently, ultimately

Mi sento un po' triste ultimamente.
I've been feeling down in the dumps lately.

Ultimamente avevo smesso di sperarci.
Lately I've stopped believing it could actually happen.

Non ho dormito molto bene ultimamente.
Recently I have not been sleeping so well.

Sara ne ha passate tante ultimamente.
Sara has been through a lot lately.

Non capisco più Giulia, ultimamente.
I don't get Giulia, ultimately.

velocemente
easily, quickly, promptly, swiftly

Quando rispondi così velocemente sembra una bugia.
Since you answered so easily, it sounds like a lie.

Posso arrivare velocemente, aspettami.
I can get there quickly, wait for me.

Slega le corde più velocemente possibile.
Untie these ropes as quickly as possible.

Vi ringrazio di essere venuti così velocemente.
Thank you for getting in here so promptly.

Il sindaco se ne occuperà velocemente.
The major will deal with it swiftly.

veramente
really, truly, actually, indeed

Questo locale merita veramente la lode.
This place really deserves the praise.

Hai veramente trasformato questa casa in un paradiso.
You truly have transformed this house into a paradise.

Viviamo in un mondo veramente meraviglioso.
We're living in a truly wonderful world.

Veramente, dobbiamo studiare.
Actually, we have to study.

È veramente raro vedere coppie felici.
It's rare indeed to see happy couples around.

verosimilmente
likely, probably, presumably, arguably, plausibly

Questo processo richiede verosimilmente alcune settimane.
This process is likely to take many weeks.

Dobbiamo ricoprire i costi, verosimilmente attorno ai 1.000 euro.
We have to cover the costs, probably around 1,000 euros.

Il quadro venne commissionato nel 1850 e verosimilmente finito
nel 1855.
The painting was commissioned in 1850 and finished presumably
in 1855.

Questi requisiti sono verosimilmente obsoleti.
These specifications arguably are out of date.

L'area residenziale era verosimilmente occupata da più famiglie.
The residential area was plausibly occupied by more than one
family.

visibilmente
visibly, clearly, noticeably, obviously

I bambini sono visibilmente nervosi per l'esame.
The children are visibly nervous about the exam.

Questi dipinti sono visibilmente diversi.
These paintings are clearly different from one another.

Usate questo prodotto per una pelle visibilmente più liscia.
Use this product for noticeably smoother skin.

Ho visto tuo fratello ed era visibilmente magro.
I've seen your brother; he was noticeably thin.

Quest'uomo soffre visibilmente.
This man is obviously in pain.

volentieri
willingly, gladly, happily, eagerly

Pensiamo di tornare volentieri, portando i nostri amici.
We plan to come back willingly bringing our friends.

Accetterò volentieri la tua richiesta.
I will gladly accept your offer.

Farebbero volentieri cambio con voi.
They would happily swap places with you.

Gliene avrei volentieri riconosciuto il diritto.
I will happily grant him the right to do so.

Gli psicologi danno volentieri consigli su come superare la
timidezza.
Psychologists eagerly give advice on how to overcome shyness.